WALKERSWOOD

CARIBBEAN KITCHEN

SIMON & SCHUSTER
A VIACOM COMPANY

First published in Great Britain by Simon & Schuster UK Ltd, 2000
A Viacom Company

5 7 9 10 8 6 4

Simon & Schuster UK Ltd, Africa House, 64–78 Kingsway, London WC2B 6AH

Text design: Rachael Hardman Carter
Cover illustration: Virginia Burke
Location photography: Joy Bell photos@joybell.com
Food photography: Steve Baxter
Home economist for food photography: Jane Stevenson
Stylist for food photography: Antonia Gaunt
Typeset by Stylize Digital Artwork
Printed in China

A CIP catalogue record for this book is available from the British Library

ISBN 0 85941 986 X

Contents

Introduction

Caribbean cooking is one of the world's great undiscovered cuisines. But more and more people are catching on! Delicious Caribbean dishes such as jerk are turning up on menus far and wide. So, if you get a chance, do accept an invitation to a Caribbean meal.

West Indian cuisine is the product of a whole range of culinary influences. The islands were originally inhabited by the Tainos and Caribs, and the settlers who succeeded them – Ashantis, Chinese, Dutch, English, French, Ibos, Indians, Irish, Spanish, Syrians and many, many more – all brought their own distinctive ingredients and customs. Before refrigeration, salted cod and mackerel were imported from Portugal and Canada and are now such staples in the diet we have almost forgotten their origins. Breadfruit was introduced by Captain Bligh from the South Sea Islands. Cassava and sweet potatoes were being used by the Tainos (indigenous Indians) when Columbus arrived.

Some Caribbean dishes are spicy and some are hot, but there is a big difference between the two. Remember that the amount of hot peppers you add to a dish is a matter of taste and can always be adjusted to your liking. The scotch bonnet – one of the hottest peppers on earth – is very often used just for its subtle flavour; it's thrown whole into the pot and not allowed to burst. Spices give flavour and mystery to our dishes. Combinations vary from island to island.

Freshly caught fish, shrimp, lobster, crab and conch provide the basis for exceptionally tasty seafood dishes. The most popular meat is chicken, followed by pork and beef. Different islands have their own meat specialities such as goat, agouti and turtle.

We have a huge variety of exotic fruits and vegetables. Some, such as papayas, bananas and pineapples, are exported extensively, but unless you have visited the islands you are not likely to know sweet-sops, naseberries, star apples or otaheities.

Because the weather is usually so delightful a lot of our cooking takes place outdoors. This means many dishes are stewed, boiled or deep fried. Street food is workman's food and tends to be oily and starchy; it relies on yams, cassava, cornmeal, green bananas, breadfruit, dasheen, flour dumplings, roti, sweet potatoes and rice.

Overall, however, Caribbean cuisine is becoming lighter and healthier and including more salads and less fat. The freshness and variety of our vegetables mean that it is easy to provide tasty and nutritious family meals.

You won't need any special cooking appliances to achieve good results with these recipes. The average Jamaican does not have a fire-pit handy, but confidently turns out a satisfactory jerk dish at home. Marinating and seasoning are often the real secret to achieving the correct depth of flavours.

There are some ingredients such as flying fish which are difficult to find, and we have substituted other foods for these. To help you identify tropical produce, some basic Caribbean ingredients are listed in the Cookpot Glossary on page 6. Or get in touch with us on the internet at www.walkerswood.com

We are sure you will enjoy cooking up a feast using these recipes. Remember to pump up the stereo with some saucy Caribbean rhythms to put you in the mood and make the table settings cheerful with the brilliant colours of some tropical blooms. You will soon find –
it's no problem.

Cookpot Glossary

Ackee

Allspice

Avocado

Mature coconut

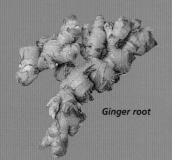
Ginger root

Ackee An unusual and delicate fruit, popular in Jamaica. Cooked and eaten as a savoury vegetable. Only the yellow part is used.

Allspice or pimento Dried fruit of the pimento tree. Flavour similar to a mixture of cloves, cinnamon and nutmeg.

Avocado Caribbean variety is larger than Californian. Think salads.

Annatto Pulp is used as orange food colouring.

Bananas, green or ripe Several varieties. Green is boiled like yam.

Breadfruit Starchy fruit. Eat boiled, roasted or fried.

Callaloo A green, leafy vegetable similar to spinach or kale. Also name of a stew in Trinidad.

Chocho or christophene Pear-shaped vegetable similar in taste to squash. Also called chayote in Latin countries.

Casareep Juice of cassava used to preserve meat in pepperpot.

Coconut The milk or cream (made from white flesh) is used in many dishes like rundown and curries. Also popular in baking. The oil is used in cooking.

Cassava Root vegetable, pounded to make flour or bammies (cakes).

Cilantro Same thing as coriander.

Escallion Similar to spring onion, but with a more pungent flavour.

Ginger Jamaican ginger is very strong and flavourful.

Guava Used for jams, meat glazes, desserts or drinks. A natural source of vitamin C.

Plantains and green bananas

Red peas

Soursop

Scotch bonnet peppers

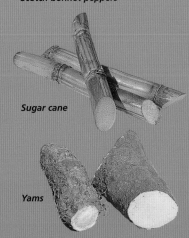

Sugar cane

Yams

Jerk Traditional method of slow-cooking highly seasoned meat over a fire-pit of pimento wood. Commercial jerk seasoning makes it easier.

Mango Many varieties. Used in ice cream, baking or salads.

Nutmeg and mace Nutmeg is grated into puddings, porridge and vegetables. Mace, nutmeg's outer covering, is used in baking.

Palm hearts Centre core of cabbage palm. A delicacy used in salads.

Plantains Looks like a big banana but should be fried, baked or boiled.

Red peas Caribbean name for red kidney beans. Very popular in rice and peas.

Scotch bonnet pepper Seriously hot pepper with a distinctive aroma. Named for its appearance.

Solomon Gundy A fish paste made with smoked herring and spices.

Soursop or guanabana Pulp is squeezed to make a very popular drink or flavouring for ice cream. Popular throughout the islands.

Sorrel Red sepals are used to make a beverage, jams or sauces. Most often seen at Christmas time.

Sugar cane Squeezed to make juice. The source of sugar and rum.

Sweet potato A Caribbean staple. Sweeter and denser than North American version.

Tamarind Sticky brown fruit in a crisp pod. Tart flesh is used for juice or as a flavouring for sauces.

Thyme Essential herb used throughout the Caribbean.

Yam Tubers with several varieties. Boiled or roasted.

Soups, Snacks & Salads

Saturday soup is a tradition. Caribbean soups tend to be hearty and can make a full and satisfying meal. Most often they are made with meat (such as pig's tail), chicken or fish, but since they also contain other strong flavours like coconut or peanut, it is easy to make tasty vegetarian versions. Most soups are not blended and contain chunks of yam, beans and vegetables and meat. Chewy flour dumplings rolled into small 'fingers' are called spinners and make a good substitute for noodles.

Snacks fill the gap before dinner. Many are designed to encourage a thirst and can be quite salty or spicy. In the islands salty chips or crisps are made from baked coconut, fried breadfruit, fried slivers of green banana or green plantains. Spicy Solomon Gundy on crackers will send you quickly to the bar. Fritters made from corned beef, salt fish, crab or conch are heartier appetizers and might be served at a cocktail party along with dishes like cold escoveitched fish and dips with avocado or salsa. Patties, (a delicious pastry casing filled with spicy ground beef, ackees or callaloo) are eaten as a lunchtime snack and are sold in many bakeries.

The most common salads are versions of coleslaw or simple combinations of lettuce, cucumber, avocado and organic tomatoes. But there is still a great variety of marinated cold lobster, crab, shrimp and conch or salads made with other exotic ingredients like palm hearts, smoked marlin, papayas, mangoes and carambola (star fruit).

Ripe ackees on a roadside stall

Red Pea Soup

'Red peas' is the commonly used name for red kidney beans in the Caribbean. This recipe can easily be converted to accommodate many other beans, such as 'gungo peas' (pigeon peas) or black beans. We have given you a vegetarian recipe here but, traditionally, both cubes of stewing beef (500g/1lb) and pickled pig's tail (250g/8oz) would be used. This is a hearty soup.

Warning! Make sure not to burst the hot pepper (remove it when stirring). For more heat, add one of Walkerswood's hot pepper sauces.

For the soup
500g/2½ cups dried red peas (red kidney beans),
    soaked overnight
2.25–3 litres/10–12½ cups water
500g/1lb yellow yam or hard yam, cut into pieces
2–3 cocos (a kind of white yam), diced
125ml/½ cup Walkerswood Coconut Milk
1 whole scotch bonnet or other hot chilli pepper

1 garlic clove, crushed
2 escallion (spring onion) stalks
1 fresh thyme sprig
salt and freshly ground black pepper, to taste

For the spinners (dumplings)
125g/1 cup plain flour
a pinch of salt

Place the red peas and water in a large pot. Allow to boil rapidly. Reduce the heat and allow peas to cook until tender (about 2 hours).

For the spinners, mix the flour and salt with enough water to make a firm dough. Roll between your hands to make pencil-sized 'snakes' and pinch off 5cm/2in lengths.

Add the yam, cocos and dumplings to the pot of red peas, along with the coconut milk, hot pepper, garlic, escallions, thyme, salt and pepper. Cook until the yam and cocos are just soft, about 30 minutes. Adjust the seasonings as necessary and remove and discard the fresh thyme stalk. Serve hot.

Serves 4–6   Preparation time: 30 minutes + soaking overnight + 2½ hours cooking

Fish Tea

The word 'tea' can refer to almost any hot, watery infusion! Some fish teas include lime juice, garlic, bay leaf, boiled green bananas and carrots.

2 litres/8¾ cups water
1kg/2¼lb red snapper or other saltwater fish,
    cleaned and scaled
1 large tomato, chopped
2 escallion (spring onion) stalks, crushed

1 whole scotch bonnet or other hot chilli pepper
1 fresh thyme sprig
salt and freshly ground black pepper, to taste
snipped fresh chives, to garnish

Place the water and fish in a large saucepan and bring to the boil. Allow to cook for 30 minutes. Add the remaining ingredients and simmer for 15 minutes. Strain before serving. Garnish with chives.

Serves 4   Preparation time: 15 minutes + 45 minutes cooking

Tomato & Sweet Potato Soup

This soup from Dominica is as delightful as it sounds. We tend to use organically grown tomatoes, which are rich in both colour and flavour. In the USA, sweet potato might be called 'sweet yam', but sweet yam is a different character in the Caribbean. Try not to get confused!

1 tbsp vegetable oil
1 tbsp butter or margarine
2 medium onions, finely chopped
225g/8oz sweet potatoes, peeled and chopped
450g/1lb tomatoes, skinned and chopped
600ml/2½ cups chicken stock
1 tsp salt

1 tsp chopped fresh thyme
juice and grated zest of 1 orange
juice and grated zest of 1 lemon or lime
freshly ground black pepper, to taste

To garnish
slices of tomato, orange and lemon or lime

Heat the oil and butter or margarine in a large saucepan. Add the onions and cook until soft. Add the rest of the ingredients and then bring to the boil. Allow to simmer for 25 minutes.
Cool. Blend the soup in a food processor and return it to saucepan. Re-heat thoroughly. Serve hot. Garnish with slices of tomato, orange and lemon or lime.

Serves 4   Preparation time: 30 minutes + 25 minutes cooking

Pumpkin Soup

Garnish this one with a dollop of sour cream or yogurt, if you like.

1 large onion, chopped
3 escallion (spring onion) stalks, chopped
25g/2 tbsp butter or margarine
1.2 litres/5 cups water
1kg/2lb peeled pumpkin flesh, coarsely chopped
3 tomatoes, skinned and chopped

150ml/generous ½ cup Walkerswood Coconut Milk
¼ tsp grated nutmeg
salt and pepper, to taste
a drop of Walkerswood Scotch Bonnet Sauce
  or Jonkanoo Sauce (optional)

Melt the butter or margarine in a medium saucepan and sauté the onion and escallions. Add the water and remaining ingredients. Bring to the boil and then simmer for 30 minutes.
Cool and blend in a food processor. Warm again before serving.

Serves 4   Preparation time: 15 minutes + 30 minutes cooking

Curried Ackee Soup

Ackees are so delicate they must be eaten or processed within hours of ripening. Canned ackees are a good substitute for fresh. Ackee, which is a very unusual fruit, is only widely eaten in Jamaica. This recipe, though delicious, is not considered a traditional dish.

1 tbsp olive oil
1 tsp Walkerswood West Indian Curry Powder
   or Curry Paste
2 escallion (spring onion) stalks, finely chopped
1 fresh thyme sprig

3 × 280g cans Walkerswood Ackees, drained
1.2 litres/2½ cups chicken or vegetable stock
a dash of Walkerswood Scotch Bonnet Pepper Sauce
   or Jonkanoo Pepper Sauce (optional)
salt and freshly ground black pepper, to taste

Heat the olive oil in a saucepan, add the curry, escallions and thyme and sauté gently. Add three-quarters of the ackees and the stock. Season with salt, pepper and Hot Pepper Sauce, to taste. Bring to the boil and simmer, uncovered, for 15 minutes. Mash the ackees into the soup to blend them, before adding the remaining whole ackees. Serve hot.

Serves 4   Preparation time: 20 minutes + 15 minutes cooking

Cream of Peanut Soup

Also called 'Sopito', this one is from St. Vincent.

50g/4 tbsp butter or margarine
1 onion, grated
1 celery stick, chopped
1 garlic clove, crushed to a pulp
leaves of 1 fresh thyme sprig, chopped
1 tbsp flour

900ml/3¾ cups chicken stock
1 cup/8oz crunchy peanut butter
475ml/2 cups milk
salt and Walkerswood Scotch Bonnet Pepper Sauce
   or Jonkanoo Pepper Sauce, to taste
1 tbsp freshly chopped cilantro (coriander), to garnish

Melt the butter gently in a large saucepan. Add the onion, celery, garlic and thyme. Cook for 3 minutes. Sprinkle in the flour, stirring constantly. Keep stirring while adding stock slowly. Increase the heat and add the peanut butter. Reduce the heat, add milk, salt and hot pepper sauce and simmer for 15 minutes. Garnish with cilantro (coriander). Serve hot.

Serves 4–6   Preparation time: 20 minutes + 15 minutes cooking

Breads & Accompaniments

Jamaican Hard Dough Bread – a soft yet dense white bread – is readily available wherever West Indians shop. It is often eaten along with soup.

Other popular accompaniments are 'Johnny Cakes', which are fried flour dumplings, or 'Festivals', which are deep-fried flour and cornmeal dumplings with a touch of sugar and salt (see page 51) and cornmeal bread.

Pepperpot Soup

Not to be confused with 'the pepperpot', which is a stew pot filled with varied ingredients. This soup is the Jamaican version, which is quite filling and could be considered a meal on its own.

250g/8oz salted beef, cubed
250g/8oz braising/stewing beef, cubed
1.5 litres/6¼ cups water
250g/8oz okra, cut into 7cm/3in pieces
1 large onion, thinly sliced
1 whole scotch bonnet or a dash of Walkerswood Scotch Bonnet Pepper Sauce or Jonkanoo Pepper Sauce
375g/12oz yellow yam, peeled and cubed

1 tsp whole cloves
1 fresh thyme sprig
2 × 535g cans Walkerswood Callaloo, drained
400ml can Walkerswood Coconut Milk
salt and pepper, to taste

To garnish
2 cooked shell-on shrimp (prawns) for each bowl (optional)

Place the salted beef and steak in a large saucepan with the water and some salt. Bring to the boil. Skim as necessary. Reduce the heat and cook for about an hour.

Add the remaining ingredients and bring back to the boil. Let simmer for about ½ hour, until the yam is soft. Check the seasoning. Garnish and serve hot.

Serves 4–6   Preparation time: 30 minutes + 1½ hours cooking

Saltfish

Saltfish or salted cod was first introduced to the islands by the Portuguese.

It is called bacalao in the Spanish-speaking islands. Nowadays it comes from Canada and is as popular as ever. There are two methods of preparing it for recipe use. As it is very dry and salty, it must be either soaked overnight or boiled two or three times (changing the water in between) until the desired level of saltiness has been reached. Tinned versions, ready to use, are available.

Stamp & Go (Saltfish Fritters)

Fritters are made about the size of the average jam-jar top. They are served with or without a spicy sauce or dip. With this basic recipe, you can substitute crab or corned beef for the saltfish.

250g/8oz dried salt cod, prepared as above
(or tinned *bacalao*, drained)
1 tsp annato oil (this is optional as it is mainly
for colour) or cooking oil
1 onion, finely chopped
125g/1 cup plain flour
1 tsp baking powder
½ tsp salt
1 egg, lightly beaten

135ml/½ cup milk or water
2½ tsp butter or margarine, melted
2 tbsp vegetable oil
½ whole scotch bonnet or other hot chilli
pepper, de-seeded and chopped, or a dash
of Walkerswood Scotch Bonnet Pepper
Sauce or Jonkanoo Pepper Sauce
vegetable oil, for frying

Drain the cod and remove all bones and skin. Flake the flesh. Heat the annato or cooking oil in a pan and sauté the onion. Set aside. Sieve the flour, baking powder and salt into a large mixing bowl. Add the beaten egg, milk or water and melted butter or margarine. Mix together well. Add the onion, 2 tbsp oil, cod and hot pepper or sauce and mix to form a batter.

Heat the frying oil in a large skillet. Use a tablespoon to drop spoonfuls of the batter into the hot oil. Cook for about 3 minutes, turning so they cook evenly to golden.

Makes about 24   Preparation time: overnight soaking + 45 minutes cooking

Solomon Gundy

This mysterious name is said to have come from the word 'Salmagundy' (from the original French salmigondis), which refers to a salad made of minced ingredients and which was popular in the court of Louis XIV. It has come a long way from there. Today it is a Jamaican speciality made with minced, smoked red herring and spices. It is certainly an acquired taste, somewhat like anchovies; you either like this strong fish paste or you don't. It is very popular on crackers, served as an appetizer, or blended with cream cheese for a dip which makes it much milder. 'Gundy', as it is familiarly known, can be tossed with penne pasta, olive oil, garlic, cilantro (coriander) and tomatoes for a quick and simple (you only cook the pasta!) dinner.

Charlie's Solomon Gundy Mussels

Mussels are not widely eaten in the Caribbean and we don't claim this recipe as being traditional, but the smoky flavour of the herring and the spices of the Gundy are such a natural complement to the mussels it works as a mysterious ingredient. This recipe, by Chef Charlie Thellusson, has been so well received, we'd like to share it.

500g/1lb live fresh mussels in their shells
1 tbsp olive oil
1 onion, finely chopped
2 garlic cloves, finely chopped
125ml/½ cup white wine

50ml/¼ cup double cream
1 tbsp finely chopped fresh cilantro (coriander) or parsley
2 tsp Walkerswood Solomon Gundy (a little goes a long way!)

Clean and prepare mussels, scrubbing well to remove the 'beards' and any barnacles and rinsing in several changes of water. Discard any that do not close when sharply tapped.

Cook the onion and garlic slowly in the oil until transparent. Add the mussels and white wine, cover and cook until the shells have opened, tossing frequently. Carefully strain off liquid (there may be grit in the bottom) into another pan and add the cream, coriander and Solomon Gundy. Re-heat.

Put the mussels in a serving dish, discarding any that have not opened and pour the sauce over the mussels. Serve immediately, with crusty bread.

Serves 2   Preparation and cooking time: 35 minutes

Escoveitch Chicken Salad

This dish can be prepared ahead and is a perfect use for leftover chicken. If you like, the pickled chicken also makes a delicious sandwich filling with the addition of a little mayonnaise. Otherwise it is a very low fat meal and simple to make.

2 boneless, skinless chicken breasts
1 tsp fresh thyme leaves
a little oil
120ml/½ cup Walkerswood Escoveitch Pickle Sauce, warmed

salt and pepper, to taste

To garnish
watercress, mixed lettuce, tomato wedges and julienned strips of sweet pepper

Preheat the grill to hot. Season the chicken breasts with thyme, salt and pepper. Brush with oil. Grill until cooked through (juices will run clear when the thickest part is pierced with a skewer).

When chicken is cool, cut into strips. Pour the warm Escoveitch sauce over chicken and chill, leaving to marinate for 10 minutes or more.

Prepare a salad platter of lettuce and watercress. Place the strips of chicken on top and decorate with the remaining garnishes. Pour a little of the marinade over before serving.

Serves 2   Preparation and cooking time: 30 minutes + 10 minutes marinating

Escoveitch

This sauce is most commonly associated with escoveitched fish (see page 41), which is similar to ceviche, except that here the fish is cooked. It is basically a spicy vinegar sauce wherein strips of onion, chocho (christophene) and carrot, plus hot pepper, thyme, garlic and pimento, have been left to pickle in a jar of vinegar. This sauce is then poured over fried fish. Walkerswood makes an excellent, easy-to-use version.

Bul Jol

This salad comes from Trinidad and gives yet another use for our beloved saltfish. It is not usually necessary to add salt to this recipe but even the best of us soak the saltfish too much from time to time, so see how it goes.

250g/8oz salt cod, prepared as described on page 17
1 lime or lemon, juiced
1 onion, finely chopped
2 eggs, hard-boiled and chopped
½ scotch bonnet or other hot chilli pepper, de-seeded and chopped, or a dash of Walkerswood Scotch Bonnet Pepper Sauce or Jonkanoo Pepper Sauce
2 tbsp finely chopped escallion (spring onion)
2 tbsp finely chopped fresh parsley

1 sweet green pepper, de-seeded and finely chopped
3 tomatoes
1 avocado

For the dressing
3 tbsp olive oil
1 tbsp white-wine vinegar
freshly ground black pepper

Place the prepared saltfish in a glass or ceramic bowl with all the ingredients except the tomatoes and avocado. Mix the dressing ingredients and add to the bowl. Mix well. Cover with cling film and place in refrigerator overnight.

When ready to serve, chop the tomatoes and halve, peel, stone and chop the avocado. Add to the salad and mix in gently.

Serve with crackers, fresh white bread or toast.

Serves about 6   Preparation time: overnight soaking + 30 minutes + chilling overnight

Palm Heart Salad

The Dominican Republic is the largest producer of palm hearts in the world. The look and texture is closest to asparagus. They are considered an exotic delicacy. Hearts of palm are also used in other types of salad.

100g can palm hearts, drained and sliced crossways
2 ripe mangoes, peeled and thinly sliced
2 ripe avocados (or 1 large), peeled, stoned
    and thinly sliced
½ cucumber, peeled and thinly sliced
½ scotch bonnet or other hot chilli pepper, de-seeded
    and finely chopped
½ lime or lemon (to be squeezed over to prevent
    avocado from discolouring)

For the dressing
½ lime or lemon, juiced
1 tsp grainy mustard
1 tbsp white wine vinegar
1 tsp sugar
4 tbsp extra virgin olive oil
salt and freshly ground black pepper,
    to taste

To make the dressing, mix the first four ingredients and then drizzle olive oil in slowly while stirring constantly. Season to taste.

Assemble all the salad ingredients in a bowl and serve the dressing on the side.

Serves 6   Preparation time: 30 minutes

Palm Heart Salad

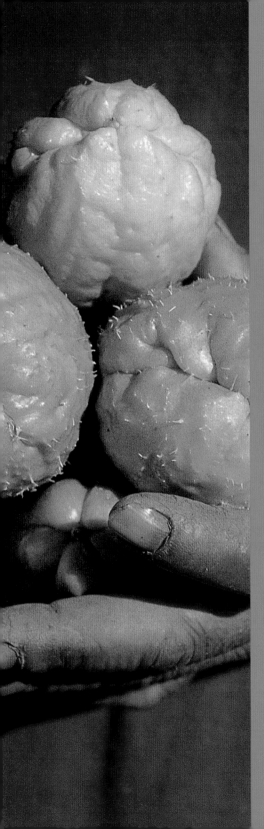

Vegetarian

With so many vegetables to choose from, vegetarian meals in the Caribbean are imaginative and flavourful.

The most obvious groups of vegetarians in the Caribbean are the Indian Hindu population in Trinidad and the Jamaican Rastafarians. Roti made with fillings of chick peas, pumpkin and potatoes are very popular wherever Indian communities are found, and the Caribbean boasts delicious vegetarian curries with flavours unique to the islands.

The Rastafarians' cooking style is called 'ital'. Their diet excludes salt, meat and chemicals; pork and shellfish are considered the most unholy foods. Food is served in as natural a state as possible and it takes a little getting used to, but the true flavours of vegetables and provisions shine through. Rastafarians use a lot of soy, coconuts and peanuts and all sorts of herbs.

The vegetarian diet can be well balanced and colourful. The best place to shop is at the vibrant Friday and Saturday outdoor farmers' markets, when freshly gathered produce has just arrived. It is a treat for more than the belly.

Some fruit like ackees and green bananas are served as vegetables. Corn is plentiful and is used for soup, breads and porridge, or is simply roasted or boiled. Cabbage, carrots, pak choy, callaloo, chocho, okras and string beans are easily found in the markets, along with many roots and tubers, like beets, yams, cassava, dasheen and coco. Fresh and dried peas and beans are sometimes still sold by the gill, measured in old-fashioned tin cups.

Job's handful of chochos

Baked Stuffed Chocho (Christophene)

This delicate vegetable is actually part of the gourd family and is close in flavour to zucchini (courgette). It is pale green in colour and pear shaped. It is usually peeled and boiled until tender and eaten simply with a little butter, salt and pepper. The seed is discarded. This recipe works well as an appetizer or side dish.

2 chochos (christophenes)

For the stuffing
1 tsp butter
½ tsp pressed or finely chopped garlic
1 onion, finely chopped
1 tsp Walkerswood Curry Paste or Powder
125g/4oz cheese, grated (use Edam, Cheddar or feta)
2 tbsp fresh breadcrumbs
salt and pepper, to taste

Preheat the oven to 180°C/350°F/Gas Mark 4. Cut each chocho in half lengthways (leave skin on). Using a large pot, place them in lightly salted boiling water and cook until just tender. Remove from water and leave until cool enough to handle. Scoop out the seed and discard. Scoop out flesh and reserve, leaving just enough to keep the (skin) shells firm.

Melt the butter in a saucepan and then add the garlic, onion, curry, reserved chocho, salt and pepper. Cook for 1 minute. Place the mixture in the chocho skins, top with cheese and then sprinkle with breadcrumbs. Place on a non-stick baking sheet then put into the oven and bake for 15 minutes or until the cheese has melted and the breadcrumb layer is just brown. Serve immediately.

Serves 4   Preparation time: 45 minutes + about 15 minutes baking

Sweet Potato & Callaloo Pie

If you are not in the Caribbean you will need to use canned callaloo greens. Another option is spinach, which is fairly similar. This is a side dish and we recommend the tomato sauce as an accompaniment. Or top this dish with grated cheese at the end and brown it under the grill.

50g/4 tbsp butter or margarine
1 onion, chopped
2 escallion (spring onion) stalks, chopped
2 garlic cloves, chopped or pressed
1 tsp chopped fresh thyme
4 tomatoes, chopped

535g/19oz can Walkerswood Callaloo, drained,
   or same amount cooked spinach
1kg/2lb sweet potato, peeled and sliced
   5mm/¼in thick
½ tsp Walkerswood Ground Allspice
salt and pepper, to taste

Preheat the oven to 180°C/350°F/Gas Mark 4. Melt the butter or margarine in a frying-pan and sauté the onion, escallions, garlic, thyme, tomatoes and drained callaloo or spinach, salt and pepper, in that order. Stir well and remove from heat. Place half the sweet potato slices in a greased baking dish. Pour on the callaloo mixture then sandwich tightly with another layer of sweet potato. Sprinkle with allspice and cover with greaseproof paper. Place in the oven and bake for about 45 minutes or until the sweet potatoes are cooked thoroughly.

Serves 4   Preparation time: 20 minutes + 45 minutes baking

Basic Tomato Sauce

2 tsp olive oil
1 escallion (spring onion) stalk, chopped
1 garlic clove, finely chopped
½ tsp fresh chopped thyme leaves
100g/3½oz tomatoes, chopped

1 tsp vinegar
1 tsp brown sugar
½ tsp Walkerswood Scotch Bonnet Pepper Sauce
   or Jonkanoo Pepper Sauce (optional)
salt and pepper, to taste

Heat the oil. Stir-fry the escallion (spring onion), garlic and thyme. Add the rest of the ingredients and simmer for 3–5 minutes. Mash with a fork or blend to incorporate the flavours. Spoon a little over each serving of Sweet Potato & Callaloo Pie.

Eggplant in Coconut Rundown Sauce

'Rundown' is the Jamaican name given to the technique of slow-cooking savoury dishes with coconut milk and spices. The most common rundown dish is Dip and Fall Back (see page 35) but this sauce is also used with vegetables. Eggplant, also known as antrober or aubergine, grows in the Caribbean. Most of our eggplant seems to be best appreciated by vegetarians.

3 medium eggplants (aubergines)
2 tbsp salt
2 tbsp olive oil
2 garlic cloves, crushed
2 tsp chopped fresh rosemary
olive oil, for frying

1 onion, sliced
6 tomatoes, roughly chopped
300ml/1¼ cups Walkerswood Rundown Sauce, or
 Coconut Milk with a dash of Walkerswood Scotch
 Bonnet Pepper Sauce or Jonkanoo Pepper Sauce
1 tsp freshly ground black pepper

Cut the eggplants into 1cm/½in slices. Sprinkle with the salt, place under a heavy weight and leave, to allow the bitter juices to come out (de-gorge), for about ½ an hour.

Rinse the eggplant slices under cold running water and pat dry with kitchen paper. Mix together the 2 tbsp of olive oil, garlic and rosemary and brush the eggplant with the mixture.

Preheat the oven to 150°C/300°F/Gas Mark 1.

In a large frying pan, heat enough olive oil for frying the aubergine, onions and tomatoes and sauté over a medium heat for 5 minutes. Add the rundown sauce or coconut milk and hot pepper sauce and heat through. Pour the mixture into an ovenproof dish and cover. Place in the oven and bake for about 20 minutes.

Serves 4–6   Preparation time: 30 minutes de-gorging + 15 minutes + 20 minutes cooking

Caribbean Vegetable Rundown

2 sweet potatoes, peeled and cubed
2 green bananas, peeled and sliced
2 chochos (christophenes), peeled and cubed
2 tbsp olive oil
2 escallion (spring onion) stalks, chopped
2 garlic cloves, crushed

6 okras, trimmed and sliced
4 tomatoes, chopped
½ tsp Walkerswood Allspice
1 tsp chopped fresh thyme
300ml/1¼ cups Walkerswood Coconut Rundown Sauce
salt and pepper, to taste

Place the sweet potatoes, bananas and chochos in a saucepan with enough water to cover. Boil for 10 minutes or until tender. Drain.

Heat the oil and then add the escallion, garlic, okras and tomatoes and stir-fry for 3–5 minutes. Add the boiled vegetables, allspice, thyme and coconut rundown sauce and cook until the sauce thickens slightly.

Serves 4   Preparation time: 20 minutes + 20 minutes cooking

Eggplant in Coconut Rundown Sauce

Stir-Fried Caribbean Vegetables with Jerk Tofu

Tofu is so bland, cooks are always looking for ways to perk it up. This recipe certainly gives it a kick and is quite hot. Use less jerk seasoning if you wish, and serve with brown rice if you want to feel especially health conscious. The key to this recipe is not to overcook the vegetables.

1 tbsp Walkerswood Jerk Marinade or Jerk Seasoning
2 tbsp palm, peanut, sesame or soya oil
500g/1lb firm tofu, or Quorn, cubed
1 onion, sliced
2 garlic cloves, finely chopped
oil, for frying

For the vegetables
about 1kg/2lb total of any combination of carrots, zucchini (courgettes), cauliflower, green cabbage, pak choy, sweet peppers and/or broccoli

Mix together jerk seasoning and oil, add to tofu and marinate for at least an hour (preferably overnight).

Heat the frying oil in a wok or suitable skillet. Deep fry the tofu cubes for 3–5 minutes and reserve. Pour out most of the oil and stir-fry the onion and garlic; then begin to add the other vegetables, hardest first. Cook very lightly; then add the tofu and stir in gently until hot. Serve immediately.

Serves 4   Preparation time: 15 minutes + 1 hour (or up to overnight) marinating + about 10 minutes cooking

Ackee & Callaloo Pasta with Feta Cheese

One step beyond macaroni and cheese! Pasta dishes are now abundant throughout the Caribbean.

250g/3½ cups penne (pasta quills) or farfalle (pasta bows)
3 tbsp olive oil
1 onion, chopped
1 escallion (spring onion) stalk, chopped
2 garlic cloves, pressed
2 tomatoes, chopped
1 tsp each chopped fresh parsley, cilantro (coriander) and thyme

535g/19oz can Walkerswood Callaloo, drained, or equal amount cooked spinach
535g/19oz can Walkerswood Ackees, drained
250g/8oz feta cheese, crumbled
salt and pepper, to taste
Walkerswood Scotch Bonnet Pepper Sauce or Jonkanoo Pepper Sauce, to taste (optional)

Cook the pasta in a large pot of boiling, salted water until *al dente* (tender but still slightly chewy).

Meanwhile heat the olive oil in a skillet and sauté the onions, escallion and garlic. Add the tomatoes and mixed herbs. Stir in the drained callaloo and toss in the ackees gently, until warm, adding salt and pepper, and hot pepper sauce, if using. Finally, add the crumbled pieces of cheese and combine everything with the hot pasta.

Serves 4   Preparation and cooking time: 30 minutes

Fish

The variety of fish and seafood found in the islands is overwhelming. We eat everything from mahimahi, flying fish and shark to calamari and sea urchin. Very important in our diet is dried saltfish, pickled herring and mackerel which can be stored without refrigeration.

It's difficult to find substitutes for Caribbean fish as tropical sea life differs from cold-water varieties in both texture and taste. Freshness is an important virtue and a reason some recipes do not travel well.

Recently a freshwater fish called tilapia has become very popular. It is similar to red snapper and is harvested in large quantities. Tilapia is available in Europe and the USA.

West Indians tend to eat the whole fish from head to tail, but if you prefer, stick to fillets or steaks.

Seafood is grilled, steamed or fried and there is a variety of Caribbean style sauces, stuffings and side dishes to complement it. Fresh limes, Bermuda onions, curry and coconut are just a few of the ingredients likely to appear around our dishes.

Many shellfish and crustaceans are marinated in vinaigrette-style seasonings and a touch of hot pepper sauce before or after cooking. They are served cold in salads.

But for a real seafood lover there is nothing to compare with a freshly caught red snapper cooked over an open fire on the beach and quickly doused with hot pickle sauce. This would be served with festival (a fried dumpling) and possibly a cold beer, and would surely send you for a nap in the shade of the nearest sea grape tree!

Fresh catch of parrot fish

Caribbean Breakfast

Throughout the islands, the tradition of a big Caribbean breakfast has remained strong. Some days it is just a large hearty bowl of cornmeal, banana or hominy corn porridge which is served with cocoa, coffee, chocolate or a variety of 'bush' teas and fruit.

Or it can be an astonishingly large meal with a choice of many types of fish dishes, sausages, liver, 'bully beef' (canned corned beef), 'cooked food' (boiled bananas, yam and dumplings), cassava cakes, tomatoes, ackees, callaloo, cabbage and avocados and, of course, bacon and eggs. Different islands have their own special combinations which are served in restaurants and these are available, if not daily, certainly on Sundays.

Dip & Fall Back

This dish of mackerel rundown (see page 31) will rarely be seen after breakfast time but it is a huge favourite in Jamaica. Serve with boiled green bananas, boiled flour dumplings and yam. A few slices of fried ripe plantain and a wedge of avocado will make it totally authentic. But don't plan to do too much for the next few hours.

1 whole pickled mackerel (about 500g/1lb)
  or shad
1 tsp vegetable oil
2 onions, chopped
3 escallion (spring onion) stalks, chopped
2 garlic cloves, chopped

3 tomatoes, chopped
3 fresh thyme sprigs
180ml/6oz jar Walkerswood Coconut Rundown Sauce
  or 200ml/¾ cup coconut milk
1 whole scotch bonnet pepper or ½ tsp Walkerswood
  Scotch Bonnet Pepper Sauce or Jonkanoo Pepper Sauce

Boil the fish in water for 15 minutes to remove excess salt. Taste for saltiness and run under cold water if necessary. Remove the skin and bones, and flake.

In a skillet, heat the oil and sauté the onions and escallions. Add the garlic, tomatoes and thyme. Mix in the rundown sauce and 50ml/¼ cup water (leave out the water if using coconut milk). Add the fish and place the whole pepper, on top, or add the hot pepper sauce. Cover and simmer for about 10 minutes. If the sauce looks too thin, simmer a little longer; if the dish looks dry, add a little more water.

Serves 4   Preparation time: 15 minutes cooking + 25 minutes cooking

Ackee & Saltfish

This dish is Jamaica's national dish. It will look surprisingly like scrambled eggs, but don't be fooled, the flavour is exceptional. Ackee and saltfish is usually a speciality breakfast dish, but quite often makes it to the lunch menu or as a dinner appetizer. Serve with boiled green bananas, yam or dumplings, fried ripe plantain and avocado. More information on ackees is on page 6 and on saltfish on page 17.

1kg/2lb salt cod, prepared as described on page 17
2 tbsp cooking oil
1 onion, chopped
2 escallion (spring onion) stalks, chopped
½ scotch bonnet pepper, de-seeded and chopped, or
    ½ tsp Walkerswood Scotch Bonnet Pepper Sauce
    or Jonkanoo Pepper Sauce

2 garlic cloves, crushed
1 tsp chopped fresh thyme
2 tomatoes, chopped
2 × 535g cans Walkerswood Ackees (about 2 dozen),
    drained
salt and black pepper, to taste

Prepare the saltfish. Heat the oil in a large frying pan, add the onion, escallions, hot pepper or sauce and garlic. Fry over low heat until the onion is transparent, then add the fresh thyme. Add the saltfish and fry, stirring constantly, for 3 minutes, and then the tomatoes and ackees. Toss gently so as not to break up the ackees. Sprinkle with salt (if necessary) and pepper before serving.

Serves 6   Preparation time: 15 minutes + 2 hours soaking + 10 minutes cooking

Blaff

A poached, marinated fish recipe from Martinique and Guadeloupe, served with rice.

4 whole, snapper, tilapia, sea bream or similar fish,
    scaled and gutted
1 lime, juiced
1.2 litres/5 cups water
2 tsp salt
1 onion, chopped

2 garlic cloves, crushed
1 tsp Walkerswood Scotch Bonnet Pepper Sauce
    or Jonkanoo Pepper Sauce
2 bay leaves
1 fresh thyme sprig
1 tsp Walkerswood Allspice

Place the fish in a bowl with half the lime juice, half the water and half the salt. Marinate for about 1 hour.

Drain and discard the marinade. Pour the remaining water into a saucepan and add the onion, garlic, hot pepper sauce, bay leaves, thyme and allspice. Bring to the boil and simmer for 5 minutes. Add the fish, cover and simmer for 5 minutes or until fish is cooked. Add the remaining lime juice and salt to taste. Serve hot.

Serves 4   Preparation and cooking time: 1 hour marination + 15 minutes

Jerk Snapper with Callaloo & Okra Stuffing

This recipe requires whole fish in order to use the stuffing to best advantage. It can be prepared in the oven or on a barbecue. It is a hot and spicy dish and works well with 'hard dough bread' (see page 15) to sop up all the juices.

2 whole snappers, tilapia or similar fish, scaled,
    gutted and cleaned (about 500g/1lb each)
1 lime, juiced
1–2 tbsp Walkerswood Jerk Seasoning or Marinade
2 tsp butter
½ tsp salt

For the stuffing
2 tbsp butter
1 onion, chopped
2 okras, chopped
535g/19oz can Walkerswood Callaloo, drained,
    or equal amount cooked spinach
¼ tsp grated nutmeg
1 plum tomato, finely chopped
salt and black pepper, to taste

Wash inside and outside the fish with lime juice. Mix the jerk seasoning or marinade with the butter and salt. Score the fish across the body with three slits and rub the seasoning mixture inside and outside thoroughly. Leave to marinate overnight or for a few hours.

Preheat the oven to 180°C/350°F/Gas Mark 4 or light the barbecue. For the stuffing, melt the butter in a hot skillet and sauté the onion and okras. Add the callaloo or spinach and the rest of the stuffing ingredients. (Make sure the callaloo is pressed quite dry so that there is not too much liquid in the stuffing.) Cook gently for about 2 minutes. Stuff the fish with the mixture and place on a large sheet of greased foil. Wrap each fish loosely but securely so that neither juices nor steam can escape. Place on a baking sheet in the oven for 15–20 minutes (depending on the size of the fish) or directly on the barbecue grill. The fish is done when it can be separated from the bone easily, but don't overcook. Open the package carefully and serve with the cooking juices.

Serves 2   Preparation time: 20 minutes + 15–20 minutes cooking + marination

Escoveitch Fish

This tangy, pickled fish dish tends to fall into three categories – breakfast, lunch or cocktail snacks – and it will be eaten hot, cold or at room temperature at any of these times. It keeps very well unrefrigerated and is quite often taken on journeys, including overseas. Customs officers in London, New York, Miami and Toronto are quite familiar with this foil-wrapped gift for family away from home! (See page 21 for more on Escoveitch.)

1kg/2lb whole fresh snapper, scaled, gutted and
   cleaned, or snapper steaks or fillets
1 lime, cut in half
salt and pepper, to taste
50g/½ cup flour, for coating
vegetable oil, for frying

For the pickle dressing
1 chocho (christophene) or cucumber, cut into strips
2 onions, sliced
2 scotch bonnet peppers, thinly sliced and de-seeded
   (optional)
180ml/6oz jar Walkerswood Escoveitch Pickle Sauce

Rub the fish with lime and rinse. Season well with salt and pepper and coat with flour. Heat the oil in a frying pan until it smokes slightly, and then fry the fish on both sides until golden brown. Arrange in a deep bowl.

Meanwhile, place the pickle ingredients in a saucepan, bring to a boil and simmer for 2 minutes. Remove from heat and pour over the fish. Allow to marinate for at least 10 minutes before serving with Bammies (cassava cakes), hard dough bread or Johnny Cakes (see page 15).

Serves 4   Preparation and cooking time: 30 minutes + 10 minutes marination

Escoveitched Salmon

Instead of frying the fish as in the above recipe, substitute freshly grilled salmon (steaks or fillets) for the snapper and continue as above. This marvellous tip came from friends in Ireland. Our humble dish is now served at banquets!

Lobster & Shrimp in Coconut Rundown Sauce

This combination is usually reserved for special occasions unless you live by the seaside where lobster and shrimp are an everyday catch.

20 large raw shrimp (king prawns), peeled and de-veined
500g/1lb lobster, shelled, flesh cubed (weight before shelling)
2 tbsp olive oil
2 escallion (spring onion) stalks, chopped
3 plum tomatoes, peeled and chopped
3 garlic cloves, crushed

½ tsp saffron strands (optional)
½ lime, juiced
2 × 180ml/6oz jars Walkerswood Coconut Rundown Sauce
2 tsp chopped fresh thyme
2 tbsp chopped fresh parsley
salt and freshly ground black pepper, to taste

Prepare the shrimp and lobster. Heat the oil in a saucepan over a moderate heat. Sauté the escallions and tomatoes and add the garlic, saffron, if using, shrimp, lobster, salt, black pepper and lime juice. Cook over high heat for 2 minutes. Reduce the heat, pour in the rundown sauce and simmer (do not allow to boil). Stir in the chopped herbs and cook for 5 minutes. Adjust the salt and pepper to taste. Serve on a bed of steamed rice, with cucumber salad.

Serves 4   Preparation and cooking time: 40 minutes

Crab Gumbo

This dish is from Antigua. A really hearty meal.

750g/1½lb cooked crabmeat
1 tbsp vegetable oil
25g/2 tbsp butter
1 onion, chopped
4 tomatoes, chopped
1 tbsp chopped fresh thyme
2 tbsp chopped fresh parsley
2 tsp Walkerswood West Indian Curry Paste
  or Powder

250g/8oz okra, trimmed and sliced
1 whole scotch bonnet pepper
600ml/2½ cups fish stock
300ml/1¼ cups Walkerswood Coconut Milk
1 tsp Walkerswood Ground Allspice
Salt and pepper, to taste

Prepare crab, if necessary. Heat oil and butter in a saucepan over moderate heat and sauté the onion. Add the tomatoes, thyme, parsley, curry paste or powder and okra and cook for 5 minutes, stirring constantly. Add the whole hot pepper, fish stock, coconut milk, allspice, salt and black pepper. Stir in the crab meat, reduce the heat and allow to simmer for 10–15 minutes.

Serves 6   Preparation time: 20 minutes + 10–15 minutes cooking

Crabmeat

Most of the Island crabs used in cooking tend to be 'land crabs'. This is a small, hard-shelled variety with delicate meat. One of the popular dishes throughout the islands is Stuffed Crab Back: the crabmeat is chopped, mixed with breadcrumbs, butter, escallion, thyme, onions, hot pepper sauce and seasoning. The mixture is stuffed into the shell with a few breadcrumbs sprinkled on top and baked in a hot oven for 10–15 minutes. It is served hot with a wedge of lemon.

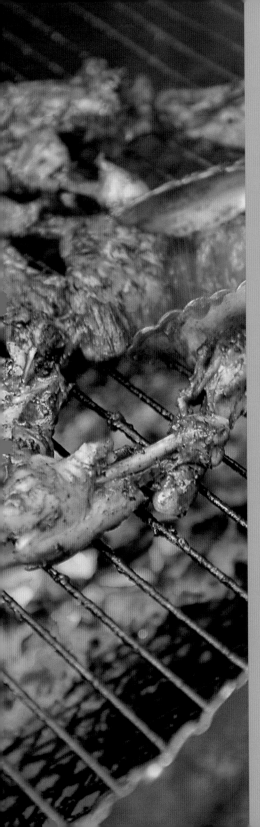

Poultry

Chicken is by far the most widely eaten main course in the Caribbean. We islanders must have perfected every possible way of preparing and enjoying it; jerked, fried, barbecued, stewed, fricasseed, roasted and curried are just a few of the methods we use.

The tastiest chicken is the free-range or common yard fowl. These are usually medium sized. Throughout the islands the preparation starts the same way: the chicken is washed and rubbed with lime and then seasoned, usually with onion, garlic, escallion, salt, pepper and thyme. It is then allowed to marinate with the seasoning. This is an essential part of getting the flavour into the bird, regardless of how you are planning to cook it. Most chicken dishes use chicken on the bone and are well cooked.

Duck and turkey, though available on the farm, are usually only seen at special occasions.

Pan-jerked chicken on Reggae Beach at Prospect, on Jamaica's North Coast

Sudden Fried Chicken

We borrowed this name which we found on a sign in a favourite fried-chicken shop in the rural hill country. It probably was not meant to be humorous! Drumettes are the first joint of the chicken wing. They look like small chicken drumsticks and are ideal for appetizers.

1.5kg/3lb chicken wings or drumettes (skin on)
vegetable oil, for deep frying

For the marinade
1 tsp garlic powder
1 tsp onion powder
1 tsp celery salt
1 tsp dried oregano

2 tsp Walkerswood Dried Jerk Seasoning
1 tsp paprika
1 tsp dried thyme
250g/2 cups flour
½ tsp ground cinnamon
2 tsp salt

Prepare chicken, wash and dry well. In a bowl, mix all the dry ingredients; coat the chicken pieces with the mixture. Lay on a flat tray and refrigerate for a minimum of 2 hours.

Heat the deep frying oil in a skillet until very hot, add the chicken pieces, in batches, if necessary, and deep fry until cooked (about 8–10 minutes).

Serves 4–6   Preparation and cooking time: 20 minutes + 2 hours marination

Chicken Rundown with Wine

6 boneless, skinless chicken breasts
1 tbsp oil
2 tbsp white wine
180ml/6oz jar Walkerswood Coconut Rundown Sauce
2 tbsp fresh cream
2 tbsp chopped fresh cilantro (coriander)
salt and pepper, to taste

For the marinade
2 garlic cloves, pressed
leaves from a big sprig of thyme
1 onion, finely chopped
1 tsp grated fresh root ginger (optional)

Wash and dry chicken and then cut into cubes. Marinate the chicken for at least 1 hour in the garlic, thyme, salt and pepper, onion and ginger, if using.

Heat the oil in a skillet. Remove the chicken and reserve the seasonings. Sauté chicken pieces until browned. Add reserved seasonings and cook for 1 minute. De-glaze the pan with wine, add the coconut rundown sauce and cream, reduce the heat and simmer for 5 minutes or until the chicken is cooked. Add the cilantro at the end. Very good with callaloo rice.

Serves 6   Preparation and cooking time: 15 minutes + 1 hour marination

Chicken Calypso

A hot, sweet and spicy dish with typical Caribbean flavours blended together. This could also be made with chunks of boneless turkey.

1 whole chicken, jointed
1 lime or lemon, halved
2 tsp butter or margarine
2 tbsp Walkerswood Guava Jelly
vegetable oil, for frying
150g/1 cup fresh cashew nuts
1 onion, chopped
1 tsp grated fresh root ginger (or to taste)

For the marinade
2 tsp salt
1 tsp Walkerswood Ground Allspice
1 tsp freshly ground black pepper
3 tbsp Walkerswood Jerk Seasoning
¼ cup white wine vinegar
1 tsp chopped fresh thyme
2 garlic cloves, pressed

Rub the chicken with the lime or lemon, rinse and pat dry. Mix together the salt, allspice, black pepper, jerk seasoning, vinegar, thyme and garlic, and press into the chicken. Leave to marinate for at least 3 hours.

Melt the butter or margarine in a saucepan, add the guava jelly and, when mixture begins to bubble, add the chicken, turning until brown.

In another saucepan, heat the oil and fry the cashew nuts, onion and ginger, mixing with a wooden spoon. Add 50ml/¼ cup of water and de-glaze the pan. Pour over the chicken and bring to a boil. Reduce the heat and simmer for 30–35 minutes. Serve with boiled rice.

Serves 6   Preparation time: 35 minutes + 3 hours marination + 30–35 minutes cooking

Jerk Chicken

Jerk is one of the most well known dishes to have travelled out of the Caribbean in recent years. Originally it was a method of preserving meat and has been traced back to the Maroons (runaway slaves in Jamaica). It falls somewhere between barbecued and smoked meat and is hot and spicy. Traditionally, the meat, (pork, chicken, etc.) is highly seasoned and placed over a fire pit of smoking pimento wood, then covered and cooked slowly. As this is highly impractical for most cooks, the development of commercial jerk seasoning with pimento spice and all the secret ingredients has made it possible to cook a decent jerk at home. (Stick to barbecue chicken if you don't like hot pepper.) You can always adjust the amount of jerk seasoning to taste, but this recipe is about where you should start! Serve with Festivals (see below).

1 whole chicken, cut in quarters (skin on)
1 lime, cut in half
1 tbsp oil
½ tsp salt

2 tbsp Walkerswood Jerk Seasoning or 3 tbsp Jerk Marinade
1 tbsp dark rum (or 2 tbsp regular rum)

Rub the chicken quarters with lime, rinse and pat dry. Sprinkle with salt. In a suitable bowl, mix the rest of the ingredients and add the chicken. Rub mixture in thoroughly and allow to marinate for at least 4 hours, preferably overnight.

Preheat the oven to 150°C/300°F/Gas Mark 1 or light the barbecue. Grill or roast the chicken slowly until very tender, for about 40 minutes.

Serves 4   Preparation time: minimum 4 hours marination + 50 minutes cooking

Festivals

Deep fried cornmeal and flour dumplings, just slightly sweet.

175g/1 cup yellow cornmeal (polenta)
125g/1 cup plain flour
2 tsp baking powder

1 tbsp sugar
½ tsp salt
oil, for deep frying

Mix all the ingredients together, adding just enough cold water to make a stiff dough. Knead and divide into six portions. Roll each portion with your hands into a log shape and squeeze lightly to flatten.

Heat the oil in a skillet or wok and deep fry the festivals until light brown, about 8 minutes each. Remove excess oil on kitchen towel before serving hot.

Makes 6   Preparation and cooking time: 30 minutes

Chicken Oriental

From Guyana, a very quick and simple dish with a deep flavour.

1.5kg/3lb chicken, cut into quarters, or boneless
   chicken breasts
120ml/½ cup soya sauce
2 tbsp brown sugar
2 garlic cloves, crushed

1 tbsp grated fresh root ginger
2 tbsp dark rum
3 tbsp white wine
170g/1 cup fresh or canned pineapple chunks, (optional)
peanut (groundnut) oil, for frying

Wash and dry the chicken pieces and place in a bowl. Put the remaining ingredients in a saucepan over moderate heat until sugar has dissolved. Allow to cool, pour over the chicken and marinate for 2 hours or overnight.

Remove chicken and reserve marinade. Brown the chicken in the oil, then reduce the heat and add the marinade and pineapple, if using. Simmer chicken breasts for 20 minutes; if using chicken quarters simmer for 45 minutes, adding extra liquid as necessary. Alternatively grill the chicken until tender.

Serves 4   Preparation time: minimum 2 hours marination + 20–45 minutes cooking

Cindy's Jerk Chicken Pasta in Creamy Sauce

A quick dinner party pleaser.

8 boneless, skinless chicken breasts
2 tbsp Walkerswood Jerk Seasoning
2 tbsp oyster sauce
250g/3½ cups penne (pasta quills)
2 tbsp olive oil
3 medium onions

160g/2 cups fresh mushrooms, sliced
6 garlic cloves, crushed
400g/14oz can evaporated milk
4 tbsp chopped fresh cilantro (coriander)
salt and freshly ground black pepper, to taste

Preheat the oven to 200°C/400°F/Gas Mark 6. Wash and dry the chicken. Season with jerk seasoning and oyster sauce and wrap each piece individually in foil. Bake for 20 minutes.

Meanwhile, cook the pasta according to packet instructions. Heat the oil in skillet and sauté the onions, mushrooms and garlic. Add the milk and salt and pepper to taste.

Cut the chicken breasts in thin strips and add these and the spicy cooking liquid (from the foil) to the milk mixture. Cook for 5 minutes to reduce liquid. Mix in the cilantro. Combine everything with the drained pasta. Serve with a salad of dressed green leaves and orange wedges.

Serves 8   Preparation and cooking time: 35 minutes

Sweet & Spicy Duck

2 duck breasts
½ tsp Walkerswood Allspice
1 tbsp grated fresh root ginger
3 garlic cloves, crushed
1 tsp lime juice

1 tsp soya sauce
2 tbsp olive oil
2 tbsp butter or margarine
2 tbsp Walkerswood Marmalade or other marmalade
salt and pepper, to taste

Wash and dry the duck breasts. Mix together allspice, ginger, garlic, lime juice, soya sauce, olive oil, salt and pepper. Score the duck breasts, place in a baking dish and marinate in the mixture for at least 1 hour.

Preheat the oven to 180°C/350°F/Gas Mark 4. Melt the butter or margarine and marmalade and pour over the duck. Place in the oven and roast for 20 minutes.

Reduce the heat to 150°C/300°F/Gas Mark 3 and cook for another 20 minutes. Serve on a bed of egg noodles or steamed rice.

Serves 4   Preparation time: 10 minutes + 1 hour marination + 40 minutes cooking

Fricassee Chicken Stewed with Tomatoes

1 whole chicken (1.5kg/3½lb), jointed
2 garlic cloves, crushed
2 tsp chopped fresh thyme
1 tsp paprika
2 tbsp cooking oil
2 onions, coarsely chopped

1 sweet pepper, de-seeded and chopped
3 tomatoes, de-seeded and chopped
1 tbsp Walkerswood One Stop Sauce
   or Pickapepper Sauce
350ml/1½ cups chicken stock
1 whole scotch bonnet or other hot chilli pepper

Wash and dry chicken. Season with salt and pepper, garlic, thyme, and paprika. Allow to marinate for 1 hour or overnight.

Heat the oil in a large, heavy pot with a lid (in the Caribbean it's called a dutchpot). Lightly brown the chicken pieces. Add the onions, sweet pepper, tomatoes and One Stop or Pickapepper sauce. Add the stock and hot pepper and bring to the boil. Reduce the heat, cover and allow to simmer until the chicken is tender, 30–40 minutes. (Don't allow the pepper to burst!) Add a little water, if necessary, as you will want to have plenty of gravy.

Serves 4–6   Preparation time: 15 minutes + minimum 1 hour marination + 30–40 minutes cooking

Meat

Local beef is popular in the islands, but it tends to be expensive. Cuts of beef are often stewed to make them tender. Ground beef or mince adds flavour to a meal where the budget is tight. Rare beef is not popular, but pickled tongue, stewed ox tail and cow foot with broad beans are all traditional dishes.

Pork is readily available and popular especially in the Spanish-speaking islands. Ham, bacon, sausages and salt pork are often used in cooking. Roast suckling pig is a big event and is sometimes prepared for a celebration. The Chinese population also eat a lot of pork.

Goat is a big favourite in Jamaica and virtually every part of the animal is used. Mannish Water, a soup made with the goat's head and other parts, is said to have aphrodisiac qualities and gives men an extra boost! Curried goat is the most popular goat dish. You can use mutton instead, but the flavour won't be the same.

Lamb is considered something of a treat in most islands as sheep are not widely reared and quite expensive. Usually only frozen New Zealand leg of lamb or chops is available in our supermarkets.

Some islanders are big fans of organ meats like liver and kidney, others not so much: it is a matter of personal taste. They are mostly eaten around breakfast time.

Wild hog, agouti, manicou and 'mountain chicken' are hunted and eaten as delicacies on some islands.

Charlie's Jerk Centre in Walkers Wood village square

Walkerswood Barbecue Ribs

The spicy version!

2kg/4lb lean pork (or beef) spare ribs

For the marinade
375ml/1½ cups Walkerswood Jerk Barbecue Sauce
¼ tsp Walkerswood Ground Allspice
1 tsp Walkerswood Jerk Seasoning
1 tsp molasses
175g/¾ cup muscovado or brown sugar
3 garlic cloves, pressed
1 tsp salt
2 tbsp dark rum

Combine all the marinade ingredients and coat the ribs. Cover and refrigerate for about 4 hours.

Light the barbecue or preheat the oven to 150°C/300°F/Gas Mark 1. Barbecue the ribs for 20–40 minutes, turning occasionally and basting with sauce. If baking, cover with foil and cook, basting occasionally, for about 1 hour.

Serves 4   Preparation time: 5 minutes + 4 hours marination + up to 1 hour cooking

Grills, Barbecues and Jerk Pans

As the weather in the islands is so conducive to outdoor cooking, we don't consider barbecuing a seasonal event. The buccaneers who roamed about the Caribbean in the eighteenth century have been credited with inventing barbecues, but we like to believe they perfected the technique, learning from the indigenous Tainos Indians.

There are many ways to get the enticing flavours of flame-cooked meat, including barbecuing a whole pig on a spit. Jerking (see page 51) is traditionally done over a covered fire pit. On the streetside, for more convenience, a jerk pan is used to grill or barbecue pork, chicken or fish. The jerk pan is simply a metal drum or barrel, cut in half, with a wire rack.

Upscale gas or coal barbecues are usually fired up on the weekend and, like everywhere else in the world, they seem to be the domain of the man of the yard. One key to successful grilling is to have the coals glowing evenly and allow time to let the food to cook slowly.

Stuffed Baked Paw-Paw (Papaya)

A similar dish is made with chocho (christophene) and you may wish to try that as an alternative. The chocho would need to be boiled first (see page 27); then continue with recipe as below. Depending on the size of the paw-paw and whether you are serving this as an appetizer or main course, you will need to decide on one or two halves per serving.

3–6 semi-ripe paw-paws (papayas), halved
    and de-seeded
50g/½ cup grated Cheddar or Edam cheese

For the stuffing
2 tbsp vegetable oil
1 onion, finely chopped
2 garlic cloves
500g/1lb lean beef or lamb, minced
    (use the best cut you can find)
1 egg, beaten
4 plum tomatoes, skinned and chopped
2 tsp Walkerswood Jerk Seasoning
1 tsp salt

Preheat the oven to 170°C/325°F/Gas Mark 3. In a large frying pan, heat the vegetable oil and sauté the onion and garlic. Mix the minced meat with the beaten egg and then fry with the onions until browned. Add the tomatoes, jerk seasoning and salt. Cook uncovered until the liquid has evaporated. Spoon the mixture into the prepared paw-paw shells and place in a suitable baking dish. Pour enough hot water around the paw-paws so that the bottom two-thirds of each shell is submerged. Bake for 45 minutes.

Sprinkle with the grated cheese and return to the heat of the oven until the cheese has melted. Serve with a mixed-leaf salad and rice.

Serves 3–6   Preparation time: 20 minutes + about 50 minutes cooking

Sautéed Beef with Onions

Most West Indians eat their meat well done, but you should cook this dish to suit your own taste. Whichever way, the recipe is quick and easy.

4 rib eye steaks, (175–250g/6–8oz each)
1 tsp white wine vinegar
50g/4 tbsp butter or margarine
1 onion, sliced thinly in rings
3 tbsp dark rum (optional)

For the marinade
2 tbsp Walkerswood Jerk Seasoning
2 garlic cloves, crushed
2 tsp salt
freshly ground black pepper, to taste

Mix together the ingredients for the marinade and use to season the steaks. Allow to marinate for at least 2 hours.

Melt the butter or margarine in a large skillet and fry the steaks on both sides for about 5 minutes for rare, 8 minutes for medium and 10 minutes per side for well done. Remove, place on a plate and keep warm.

Place the onions in the skillet and cook for a few minutes. De-glaze with the rum and then return the steaks to the pan and toss with the onions. Serve with a green salad.

Serves 4   Preparation time: minimum 2 hours marination + about 25 minutes cooking

Cacique Burger

The Cacique was the chieftain or king of the Tainos Indians. He traditionally wore an elaborate headdress. This is the king of burgers! The recipe is so delicious you will forget about the fast kind. The pineapple is optional.

2 tbsp vegetable oil
1 large onion, finely chopped
2 garlic cloves, crushed
1 green sweet pepper, de-seeded and finely chopped
1kg/2lb lean beef, freshly minced
1 tsp dried mixed herbs
2 eggs, beaten

2 tbsp Walkerswood Barbecue Sauce or One Stop Sauce
125g/1 cup fresh breadcrumbs
salt and pepper, to taste

To serve
10 fresh pineapple rings, peeled and cored (optional)
melted butter, for basting
10 hamburger buns

Place the vegetable oil in a saucepan, heat, add the onion, garlic and pepper and sauté for 3 minutes.

Transfer the mixture to a large bowl and mix in the beef, herbs, eggs, sauce and breadcrumbs. Season with salt and pepper. Form into 10 patties and allow to rest in fridge for 30 minutes.

Grill over a hot heat for 5 minutes on each side. Meanwhile, place the pineapple slices on the grill, brush with melted butter and cook for 3–6 minutes on each side. Serve each burger on a bun, topped with the pineapple, and your favourite relish or topping.

Serves 10   Preparation and cooking time: 40 minutes + 30 minutes resting

Curried Goat

This dish is a huge favourite in Jamaica but causes some consternation where goat is not commonly eaten. For that reason, we suggest mutton as a substitute for goat, as it is the closest in flavour. West Indian curry powder is a unique blend and we recommend that you try to find some for this recipe.

1.5kg/3lb goat leg and ribs, or mutton, chopped
   into small pieces (including bone)
1 tbsp salt
2 garlic cloves, crushed
1 lime or lemon, juiced
1 onion, sliced
50g/2oz Walkerswood West Indian Curry Powder
   or Paste
1 beef tomato, chopped

½ tsp Walkerswood Scotch Bonnet Pepper Sauce
   or a scotch bonnet, de-seeded and chopped
1 tbsp chopped fresh thyme
1 tsp freshly ground black pepper
½ tsp Walkerswood Ground Allspice or whole allspice
   (pimento) berries, crushed
2 escallion (spring onion) stalks, chopped
½ tsp finely chopped fresh root ginger (optional)
2 tbsp vegetable oil

Wash the prepared goat meat and dry. Mix together all the ingredients except the oil and rub into the meat. Leave to marinate for at least 2 hours.

Remove any large pieces of seasoning from the meat (onions, escallions, allspice berries etc.) and reserve. In a large skillet, heat the oil over a medium heat and add the meat. Brown, turning the pieces often to seal in flavours. Lower the heat, return the reserved seasoning to the pan and add about 450ml/2 cups of water. Cover and allow to simmer until the meat is tender (about 1½ hours). Add a little extra water, if necessary, as you will need some gravy. Simmer for 30 minutes more.

Serves 6   Preparation time: minimum 2 hours marination + 20 minutes + 2 hours cooking

Jerk Lamb with Guava Sauce

This recipe comes from the divine restaurant at Strawberry Hill in Jamaica. It is such a wonderful dish we reserve it for special occasions. With this dish the heat from the jerk seasoning remains on the outside of the roast and most people will consider it spicy but not hot. Allow the full time for marination so that you get the best results. Serve this meal with creamed white yam or potatoes and steamed chocho.

2.5kg/5lb boned leg of lamb or lamb cutlets
3 tbsp Walkerswood Jerk Seasoning
   (less if using cutlets)
2 tsp salt or to taste

For the sauce
1 head unpeeled garlic
175g/6oz Walkerswood Guava Jelly
   or redcurrant jelly
50ml/3 tbsp white wine vinegar
1 tsp chopped fresh parsley
1 tsp chopped fresh cilantro (coriander)

Rub the salt and jerk seasoning into the lamb thoroughly. Cover and marinate in the fridge overnight.

Preheat the oven to 180°C/350°F/Gas Mark 4. Roll up and tie the leg lamb in three places to secure. Roast for 45 minutes (medium rare) or about 15 minutes more for well done lamb. If using cutlets grill for 8–10 minutes on both sides. Roast the head of garlic for about 45 minutes.

Crush the soft insides of the garlic cloves into a saucepan. Add all the other ingredients for the sauce and stir. Bring to the boil, making sure the guava jelly has melted completely. Simmer and allow to reduce by half.

Allow the lamb to rest for 10 minutes before carving. Slice the lamb and glaze with the warm sauce.

Serves 8–10 Preparation time: 15 minutes + overnight marination + 45–60 minutes cooking

Curried Meatballs in Spicy Coconut Rundown

As mince is readily available, meatballs are quite popular in the Caribbean, seasoned in various ways. This version is good and spicy and brings together the richness of both curry and coconut. Serve this with callaloo rice (steamed white rice with chopped callaloo and a little coconut milk) or roti.

1 tbsp vegetable oil
2 garlic cloves, chopped
1 tsp Walkerswood Ground Allspice
1 tsp brown sugar
3 beef tomatoes, chopped
2 escallion (spring onion) stalks, chopped
180ml/6oz jar Walkerswood Coconut Rundown Sauce
   or Coconut Milk

For the meatballs
2 tbsp butter or margarine
1 large onion, finely chopped
500g/1lb lean beef, minced
1 egg
3 tbsp breadcrumbs
2 tsp salt
1 lime or lemon, juiced
1 tsp ground coriander
1 tsp Walkerswood Scotch Bonnet Pepper Sauce
   or Jonkanoo Pepper Sauce
2 tbsp Walkerswood West Indian Curry Powder
   or Paste

Place a skillet over moderate heat and add the butter or margarine. When melted, add the onion and cook for a minute. Add this to the beef, egg, breadcrumbs, salt, lime or lemon juice, coriander, hot sauce and curry in a mixing bowl. Stir well together. Shape into about 12 meatballs. Heat the oil in the skillet and fry the meatballs until cooked, for 10–15 minutes. Remove and keep warm.

To the skillet, add the garlic, allspice, sugar, tomatoes and escallions and sauté for 5 minutes. Add the rundown sauce or coconut milk and cook for 5 more minutes. (If using coconut milk, cook longer, to reduce.) Add the meatballs to the sauce and heat through.

Serves 4   Preparation and cooking time: 40 minutes

Essential Side Dishes

Rice & Peas

Sunday dinner would never be the same without this dish. It goes by a variety of names: in Trinidad it is Peas and Rice; in Spanish speaking islands such as Cuba it is Moros y Cristianos; and in the French-speaking islands like Haiti, it is Riz et Pois Colles. They are all Caribbean bean and rice dishes with slight variations of beans and seasonings. This is the Jamaican version. You will enjoy the smell as it cooks.

250g/1 cup dried red peas (red kidney beans),
   soaked overnight
350ml/1½ cups Walkerswood Coconut Milk
3 escallion (spring onion) stalks, chopped

1 fresh thyme sprig
salt and freshly ground black pepper, to taste
400g/2 cups uncooked white rice
1 whole scotch bonnet

Place beans in a large, heavy saucepan with a lid. Add enough water to cover and boil until just tender, about 2 hours.

Add the coconut milk and seasonings and then the rice. Top up with water, if necessary, so that there is about 2½ times as much liquid as rice and beans. Place the hot pepper on top and bring to the boil. Reduce the heat and cover. Let the rice steam slowly for about 25–30 minutes or until all the liquid is absorbed and the rice is tender. Do not stir while cooking or allow the pepper to burst! Remove the pepper and thyme stalk, then fluff lightly before serving.

Serves 6   Preparation time: 15 minutes + about 2¼ hours cooking

Fried Plantain & Boiled Ground Provisions

Plantains are like overgrown bananas but should be cooked. They are ripe when the skins are very mottled or black. Unripe (or green) plantains can also be fried but are not sweet. Twice-fried green plantains are called tostones, banane pese or patacones and are pressed flat before re-frying. Boiled ground provisions are good with butter or gravy.

For fried plantain, remove plantain skins by trimming both ends and making a slit down one side before peeling the skin away. Cut into slices or diagonals about 5mm/¼in thick. Fry in vegetable oil, turning until both sides are slightly brown. Allow excess oil to be absorbed by kitchen paper. Serve hot.

Baked, whole ripe plantain is easy. Remove the skin, grease with a little oil and bake along with your chicken or main dish for about 25 minutes.

For boiled ground provisions, trim the ends of green bananas and slit the skin lengthways on two sides. Boil in salted water for 10–15 minutes. Remove skin before serving. Keep in pot water until ready to eat. Peel yams and sweet potatoes and cut in thick slices. Place in large pot of salted, boiling water and cook for about 15–20 minutes until your fork says they are ready.

Desserts & Drinks

The Caribbean is known for its fabulous variety of unusual fruit so it stands to reason that our desserts and beverages reflect that bounty. Home-made ice creams come in more fruit and spice flavours than commercial brands.

Popular dessert flavours come from local vanilla, banana, guava, allspice, pineapple and coconut. Bread pudding, rum cake, custards and flans are all great favourites. Some traditional desserts, like duckanoo and sweet potato pudding, are made from sweet potatoes.

Caribbean drinks are truly exotic and have names to match. With the burgeoning tourist trade they are in high demand. The region boasts a wide range of internationally famous brands of rum like Appleton, Bacardi, Barbancourt and Mount Gay, and beers such as Red Stripe and Carib. Top quality liqueurs such as Tia Maria and Curacao are from the Caribbean. Locals create and consume home-made drinks like ginger wine and pimento liqueur. Many of these drinks are used to flavour desserts. Fresh ginger beer, sorrel, soursop, cane, tamarind, june plum juice and peanut punch are quite common.

Sweets for the sweet!

Sweet Potato Pudding

This is an old-time favourite, a very solid pudding.

1kg/2lb sweet potatoes, peeled and grated
1 medium coco (a kind of white yam),
    peeled and grated (optional)
750ml/4 cups coconut milk
75g/3oz raisins
1 tsp vanilla essence

½ tsp grated nutmeg
125g/½ cup brown sugar

For the topping
250ml/1 cup Walkerswood Coconut Milk
125g/½ cup sugar
25g/1oz raisins

Preheat the oven to 180°C/350°F/Gas Mark 4. Mix the grated sweet potato and coco with the coconut milk, raisins, vanilla, nutmeg and sugar. The mixture should be runny. Pour into a buttered baking dish or pan about 23cm (9 inches) in diameter. Place in the oven for 1 hour or until the top is hard.

Mix the topping ingredients together and pour over the pudding. Bake for another 20 minutes or until a knife inserted in the middle comes out clean. The top will be softer. Serve hot or cold.

Serves 12–14 Preparation time: 15 minutes + about 1 hour 20 minutes cooking

Coconut Gizzadas

These are open pastry tarts, often made pink with food colouring.

170g/2 cups unsweetened dessicated coconut
    (or 1 mature coconut, grated)
225g/1 cup brown sugar
¼ tsp grated nutmeg

2 tsp almond extract
1 tbsp water
1 quantity shortcrust pastry (see page 75)

Mix the filling ingredients and heat over a low flame until softened, about 15–20 minutes. Preheat the oven to 180°C/350°F/Gas Mark 4.

Divide the pastry into about eight pieces. Roll into balls and flatten. Using a pastry cutter or the rim of an average tumbler, cut circles. Pinch the edges to form a rim. Place on a greased baking sheet and bake the pastry shells for 8 minutes.

Fill the shells with the coconut mixture and then bake for a further 15–20 minutes, until the pastry is just brown on the edges.

Makes 8   Preparation time: 30 minutes + 15–20 minutes cooking

Spice Bun & Butter Pudding

Bread pudding with a difference.

250g/8oz spice bun (available where
   West Indians shop)
350ml/1½ cups milk
250ml/1 cup Walkerswood Coconut Milk
1 tsp vanilla essence

¼ tsp grated nutmeg
50g/¼ cup sugar
2 eggs, beaten
butter, at room temperature, for spreading

Preheat the oven to 180°C/350°F/Gas Mark 4. Cut the bun into thin slices. Butter each slice. Grease a loaf pan (tin) and layer slices of bun in it. In a bowl, mix the milk, coconut milk, vanilla, nutmeg, sugar and eggs. Mix well. Pour this mixture over the bun and bake for about 45 minutes. Serve at room temperature.

Serves 2–4   Preparation time: 10 minutes + 45 minutes cooking

Mango Fool

350g/12oz flesh from fresh ripe mango, chopped
300ml/½ pint double cream
½ tsp vanilla essence

3 tbsp icing sugar
fresh sprigs of mint, to garnish

Put the mango chunks in a blender or liquidiser and blend. Whip together the cream, vanilla essence and 2 tbsp icing sugar. Chill mango and cream separately for at least an hour. Just before serving fold the two together. Divide between four serving bowls or glasses. Sprinkle with remaining icing sugar and garnish with mint.

Serves 4   Preparation time: 15 minutes + chilling

Guava Pie

12 small ripe guavas or mango or otaheite apple slices   2 × quantity of shortcrust pastry (see below)
450ml/scant 2 cups water   1 beaten egg
125g/½ cup brown sugar

Peel the guavas or mango, but leave skin on otaheite, cut in half, remove seeds and discard them. Mix the water and sugar in a saucepan and add the fruit. Cook for about 10 minutes. Remove the fruit, set aside and allow liquid to boil until it reduces to a syrupy consistency. Preheat the oven to 200°C/400°F/Gas Mark 6.

Line a 23cm/9in flan ring or pastry dish with half the rolled out shortcrust pastry and fill with the fruit. Pour the syrup over and then cover with pastry. Seal the edges and make three slits in the top, to allow the steam to escape. Glaze with beaten egg. Bake for 10 minutes.

Lower the oven heat to 180°C/350°F/Gas Mark 4 and continue cooking until the top is golden (about another 30 minutes).

Serves 6   Preparation time: 30 minutes + 40 minutes cooking

Shortcrust Pastry

225g/2 cups plain flour   a pinch of salt
125g/4oz cold butter, cut in small pieces   3–6 tbsp iced water

Sieve the flour and salt together, add the butter and combine by rubbing in until the mixture resembles breadcrumbs. Pour in a spoonful or so of iced water, mixing in a little at a time until a firm dough is formed. It should not be sticky. It should be prepared at least half an hour before you want to use it. Wrap in cling film and refrigerate until ready to use.

Makes enough to line a 20cm/8in flan tin Preparation time: 10 minutes + chilling

Baked Bananas

Make as many as you wish using this basic ratio of bananas to other ingredients. (They shrink!)

4 ripe bananas, peeled   250ml/1 cup orange juice
4 tbsp brown sugar   1 tbsp rum
4 tsp butter   4 tbsp coconut cream or ice cream, to serve

Preheat the oven to 180°C/350°F/Gas Mark 4. In a greased baking dish, place the bananas, sprinkle with sugar and place a little butter on top. Mix the orange juice and rum and pour around the bananas. Bake for 20 minutes. Serve each one with a dollop of coconut cream or ice cream.

Serves 4   Preparation time: 5 minutes + 20 minutes cooking

Guinness Punch

As served at Bamboula restaurant in Brixton, London. It may sound strange but it is very popular!

4 bottles Guinness
250ml/1 cup milk
1 tbsp vanilla essence

½ tsp grated nutmeg
397g can sweetened condensed milk or to taste

Combine the first four ingredients. Add the sweetened condensed milk little by little, until it is to your taste. Chill before serving.

Serves 6–8   Preparation time: 5 minutes + chilling

Ginger Beer

125g/4oz fresh root ginger, peeled and grated
2.5 litres/10 cups water
2 limes, juiced

1kg/4 cups sugar
2 whole cloves

Place all ingredients in a large, non-reactive saucepan. Bring to the boil and boil for 5 minutes. Remove from the heat and allow to stand overnight.
   Strain through a sieve and check the sweetness. Pour into bottles and allow to stand for 5 days before drinking. Chill before serving.

Serves 6   Preparation time: 10 minutes + overnight standing + 5 days maturing + chilling

Rum Punch

Remember the ditty and you will get the ratio right every time! 'One of sour, two of sweet, three of strong and four of weak!' We would not dare to suggest how many this amount serves! Go easy.

250ml/1 cup fresh lime juice ('sour')
450g/2 cups brown sugar ('sweet')
750ml/3 cups Appleton rum ('strong')
4 cups water ('weak') or tropical fruit juice (use less
   sugar if using fruit juice, as you will be adding
   extra sweetness)
crushed ice

To serve
Angostura bitters, freshly grated nutmeg,
   slice of lime, orange or fresh pineapple,
   Maraschino cherries

Mix all the punch ingredients in a large bowl and chill. Serve in glasses and finish up each drink with a few dashes of Angostura bitters, freshly grated nutmeg and a slice of lime, orange or fresh pineapple and the traditional cherry on top. Serve over ice.
   It gets better by the hour, so make it ahead and keep refrigerated.

Guinness Punch, Ginger Beer and Rum Punch

General index

Recipe index

About Walkerswood

What began in the village of Walkers Wood 21 years ago as a rural community's effort to create employment for its people, has grown into a Caribbean food manufacturing company with an international brand name and a strong demand for its products.

Based in the cool green hills of the St. Ann district of Jamaica, 14 kilometres from the famous tourist beach resort of Ocho Rios, Walkerswood Caribbean Foods now produces a wide range of authentic sauces, seasonings and condiments.

The company remains employee-owned and is a source of both pride and income in the community. With approximately 60 employees it has an impact on hundreds of farmers island-wide who supply the factory with raw materials.

Before the early morning mist has evaporated the factory is already a hive of activity. Freshly picked spices and produce are being unloaded and a new day has begun for the Walkerswood team.

WALKERSWOOD PRODUCTS ARE AVAILABLE IN BOTH RETAIL AND CATERING SIZES.

Website **www.walkerswood.com**

HEAD OFFICE
Walkerswood Caribbean Foods Ltd
Walkers Wood PO, St Ann, Jamaica WI
Tel (876) 917 2318-9
Fax (876) 917 2648
Email wcfoods@cwjamaica.com

Walkerswood Marketing (Europe) Ltd
Bramfield Road, Wenhaston, Suffolk IP19 9EA UK
Tel (01502) 478147
Fax (01502) 478150
Email wwoodeur@aol.com

Walkerswood Marketing (North America) Inc
6187 NW 167th Street (unit H29), Miami, Florida 33015 USA
Toll free 1 800 827 0769
Tel (305) 556 4715
Fax (305) 556 5879
Email wwoodna@bellsouth.net

Catering & Restaurant, Bamboula Jerk Kitchen
12 Acre Lane, Brixton, London SW2 5SG UK
Tel (0207) 737 6024
Fax (0207) 737 4336
Email info@bamboula-restaurant.co.uk